In Loving Memory Of

_____

Those we love can never
really leave us.

They live on through our
memories and in our hearts.

Name

Thoughts & Messages

Name

Thoughts & Messages

_____

_____

_____

Name

Thoughts & Messages

Name

Thoughts & Messages

_____

_____

_____

_____

_____

_____

_____

_____

_____

_____

_____

Name

Thoughts & Messages

Name

Thoughts & Messages

Name

Thoughts & Messages

_____

_____

_____

Name

Thoughts & Messages

Name

Thoughts & Messages

Name

Thoughts & Messages

_____

_____

_____

_____

_____

_____

_____

_____

_____

_____

Name

Thoughts & Messages

Name

Thoughts & Messages

Name

Thoughts & Messages

_____

_____

_____

_____

_____

_____

_____

_____

_____

_____

_____

Name

Thoughts & Messages

Name

Thoughts & Messages

Name

Thoughts & Messages

Name

Thoughts & Messages

_____

_____

_____

_____

_____

_____

_____

_____

_____

Name

Thoughts & Messages

Name

Thoughts & Messages

Name   Thoughts & Messages

_____   _____

                                       _____

                                       _____

_____   _____

                                       _____

                                       _____

_____   _____

                                       _____

                                       _____

Name

Thoughts & Messages

Name

Thoughts & Messages

Name

Thoughts & Messages

Name

Thoughts & Messages

Name

Thoughts & Messages

Name

Thoughts & Messages

Name

Thoughts & Messages

Name

Thoughts & Messages

Name

Thoughts & Messages

Name

Thoughts & Messages

Name

Thoughts & Messages

Name

Thoughts & Messages

Name

Thoughts & Messages

Name

Thoughts & Messages

Name

Thoughts & Messages

Name

Thoughts & Messages

Name

Thoughts & Messages

Name

Thoughts & Messages

Name

Thoughts & Messages

Name

Thoughts & Messages

Name

Thoughts & Messages

Name

Thoughts & Messages

Name

Thoughts & Messages

Name   Thoughts & Messages

_____   _____

                                        _____

                                        _____

_____   _____

                                        _____

                                        _____

_____   _____

                                        _____

                                        _____

Name

Thoughts & Messages

Name

Thoughts & Messages

_____

_____

_____

_____

_____

_____

_____

_____

_____

Name

Thoughts & Messages

Name

Thoughts & Messages

Name
Thoughts & Messages

Name

Thoughts & Messages

_____

_____

_____

_____

_____

_____

_____

_____

_____

_____

_____

Name   Thoughts & Messages

Name

Thoughts & Messages

Name

Thoughts & Messages

_____

_____

_____

_____

_____

_____

_____

_____

_____

_____

_____

Name

Thoughts & Messages

Name

Thoughts & Messages

Name

Thoughts & Messages

_____

_____

_____

Name

Thoughts & Messages

Name

Thoughts & Messages

Name

Thoughts & Messages

Name

Thoughts & Messages

Name

Thoughts & Messages

_____

_____

_____

_____

_____

_____

_____

_____

_____

_____

_____

Name

Thoughts & Messages

_____

_____

_____

_____

_____

_____

_____

_____

_____

_____

Name

Thoughts & Messages

_____

_____
_____
_____

_____

_____
_____
_____

_____

_____
_____
_____

Name

Thoughts & Messages

_____

_____

_____

_____

_____

_____

_____

_____

Name

Thoughts & Messages

Name

Thoughts & Messages

Name

Thoughts & Messages

_____

_____

_____

_____

_____

_____

_____

_____

_____

_____

Name

Thoughts & Messages

Name

Thoughts & Messages

Name

Thoughts & Messages

Name

Thoughts & Messages

Name

Thoughts & Messages

Name

Thoughts & Messages

_____

_____

_____

_____

_____

_____

_____

_____

_____

_____

_____

_____

Name

Thoughts & Messages

Name   Thoughts & Messages

_____   _____

                        _____

                        _____

_____   _____

                        _____

                        _____

_____   _____

                        _____

                        _____

Name

Thoughts & Messages

Name

Thoughts & Messages

_____

_____

_____

Name

Thoughts & Messages

Name

Thoughts & Messages

Name

Thoughts & Messages

Name

Thoughts & Messages

Name

Thoughts & Messages

_____

_____

_____

_____

_____

_____

_____

_____

_____

Name

Thoughts & Messages

Name

Thoughts & Messages

Name

Thoughts & Messages

Name

Thoughts & Messages

Name   Thoughts & Messages

_____

_____

_____

Name

Thoughts & Messages

_____

_____

_____

Name

Thoughts & Messages

Name

Thoughts & Messages

_____

_____

_____

_____

_____

_____

_____

_____

_____

_____

_____

Name

Thoughts & Messages

Name

Thoughts & Messages

Name

Thoughts & Messages

Name   Thoughts & Messages

Name

Thoughts & Messages

Name

Thoughts & Messages

Name

Thoughts & Messages

Name   Thoughts & Messages

Name

Thoughts & Messages

_____

_____

_____

_____

_____

_____

_____

_____

_____

_____

_____

Name

Thoughts & Messages

Made in the USA
Monee, IL
24 January 2022